UNDERSTANDING

the

POWER

of

GOD'S WORD

M. J. Welcome

i|Page

Other Books by M. J. Welcome

Spiritual Diseases of the Unbridled Tongue

The 21-Day Crucifixion Challenge

Overcome Secret Sins in 15 Days

Battling for the Light

SMART PUBLISHING HOUSE
A Division of MDW Consulting Group
Far Rockaway, New York
www.smartpublishinghouse.com

Editing | Layout S.M.A.R.T Copy Designs
Proofreaders | Mary Ball | Matteel Welcome
S.M.A.R.T Copy Designs
www.smartcopydesignsinc.com

First Published by Smart Publishing House
08/08/16

Library of Congress Control Number: 2016911599
ISBN 10-0-9978268-0-0
ISBN 13-978-0-9978268-0-7

Scripture quotations are from the Holy Bible, King James Version unless otherwise specified. Hebrew and Greek meanings from Strong's Concordance.

Printed in the U.S.A

TABLE OF CONTENTS

APPRECIATION

Father, we thank you for the new season you have led us into. We thank you that our eyes are being opened and our ears are able to hear the words that you whisper to our spirits.

Lord, your word says that those who know their God can do great exploits. Father, we thank you that we are getting to know you more and more.

"And such as do wickedly against the covenant shall he corrupt by flatteries: but the people that do know their God shall be strong, and do exploits." Daniel 11:32

We call forth great exploits in this season, in the name of Jesus, amen.

Special thanks to my friend Mary L. Ball, a gifted and talented writer, who

helped proofread this book. May the Lord continue to richly bless you!
To my son Matteel. I thank you for your hard work in proofreading each new manuscript without complaint. May the Lord bless you for investing your time and energy to help your mother!

Dwain, thank you for all your support and encouragement. Thank you for investing the time with the Lord to study whatever the Lord moves me do. There is power in one and I thank God that you and I are one in the Lord.

INTRODUCTION

"My people are destroyed for lack of knowledge: because thou hast rejected knowledge, I will also reject thee, that thou shalt be no priest to me: seeing thou hast forgotten the law of thy God, I will also forget thy children." Hosea 4:6

In the book of Hosea, the Lord reveals that his people perish because they lack knowledge. The knowledge referred to is perception, discernment, wisdom and understanding.

It is a knowledge that is rooted in the ability to distinguish one thing from another, being able to discriminate between that which is good and that which is evil, it is knowing, or learning to know. In essence, God was speaking to their inability to distinguish between God's ways and those of the world. They could not perceive the difference. Their inability made them unwise and easy targets for the enemy.

Knowledge was available to them, but they chose to reject it. Therefore, they chose to perish.

Understanding the Power of God's Word reveals the depth, wealth and ability of God's word to accomplish all that he sends it forth to do.

It is my earnest hope and desire that as you read each lesson you will discover something new about the **power** of God's Word. I pray new opportunities will be opened for you so you can apply the word to it. I call forth *change* for you. May the word of God *change* everything that you thought you knew and open unto you what God desires for you to know about him.

May the word of God pierce through all darkness and usher you into greater light in the name of Jesus.

Be blessed for you are highly favored, amen.

M. J. Welcome

POWER

GOD'S WORD

"But he answered and said, It is written, Man shall not live by bread alone, but by every word that proceedeth out of the mouth of God." Matthew 4:4

To live is to be alive. It is breathing, being active, to be full of life. It is **zaō**. It means "to have true life and to be worthy of the name" according the Strong's Concordance.

God wants us to live *true* lives because the devil has shrouded us in darkness. He has covered us in shadows. He has presented us with things that appear to be real, true, and genuine living and it is not.

If we want to really, live the way God intended from the beginning, it starts with comprehending the worth and value of each word that exits the mouth of God!

There is power wrapped up in God's words. It goes beyond our natural comprehension. It is capable of securing the fullness of life that God proposed for us. The question each of us must answer is are we willing to live by more than mere bread? Are we willing to live by the very Word of God?

DAY 1

THE RHEŌ OF GOD'S WORD

"He that believeth on me, as the scripture hath said, out of his belly shall flow rivers of living water." John 3:38

The Hebrew word **rheō** means to flow. *Rheō* is the same word for *speak* which means to pour forth or to utter. God's Word when spoken accomplishes all that it is set forth to do for it causes things to be brought into existence.

"Now all this was done, that it might be fulfilled which was spoken G4483 of the Lord by the prophet, saying," Matthew 1:22

God's Word waters and shines light where it is sent for his pleasure and delight (Romans 9:15). God operates according to his own counsel. All that he does is geared to perpetuating his character and nature throughout creation. He began this work in the beginning and it will continue until he has accomplished what he intended.

*"And a **river** went out of Eden to water the garden; and from thence it was parted, and became into four heads. The name of the first is Pison: that is it which compasseth the whole land of Havilah, where there is gold;" Genesis 2:10-11*

In the beginning, a river flowed from Eden. The Hebrew word *nahar* means river, or stream, but its core meaning is to burn, shine, to beam, to flow, or to be light. The *nahar* of God flowed from a place of pleasure and delight. From a single source, it was divided into four chief parts in order to shake the earth. The first part was called *Pison,* which means increase, to spring about, or to be spread.

Pison was sent forth to bring about change in the land of *Havilah* which means circle. It was to encircle the land and cause it to change direction according to meaning of the word *compasseth* (*cabab*) in Genesis 2:11. God sent forth *Pison* in order to get *Havilah* to turn itself or to transform itself.

The root meaning of the word **havilah** is to twist, fear, dance, whirl, writhe, and tremble, to be in anguish, to be distressed or to be pained. This indicates that *Pison* was endowed with the ability to cause change through the use of many modalities. The purpose was to bring forth that which God desired and longed for.

Havilah was a rich place since gold was found in the location. It was a place of brilliance and splendor. It was a place that shimmered. *Havilah* possessed several types of precious materials including onyx (blanched) gemstones and bdellium (gum resin). These materials were precious for they underwent a process of color extraction. They were made white through bleaching. This indicates that as we submit to the process of God he will cleanse and refine us to become precious gems of righteousness (Revelation 3:18).

"Come now, and let us reason together, saith the LORD: though your sins be as scarlet, they shall be as white as snow; though they be red like crimson, they shall be as wool." Isaiah 1:18

Pison foreshadows the work of Holy Spirit in our lives. As we allow the Word of God in conjunction with the Spirit of God to flow in our lives we will undergo a bleaching process. We will turn on ourselves. We will judge our old nature false and be established in our new nature through the completed work of Christ. The same way that *Pison* circled *Havilah* we are to allow the power of God to encircle us.

"And the name of the second river is Gihon: the same is it that compasseth the whole land of Ethiopia." Genesis 2:13

The second river was called **Gihon**, which means to burst forth. It includes being drawn or being brought forth.

Gishon circled Ethiopia. Ethiopia is linked with Cush, which means black. Out of Ethiopia (blackness), *Gishon* was to cause something to be brought forth.

Each person has sinned and fallen short of the glory of God (Romans 3:23). The penalty for our crime is death (Romans 6:23). But God in his mercy sent forth *Gishon* for us which brought us out of darkness and into light.

"For ye were sometimes darkness, but now are ye light in the Lord: walk as children of light: (For the fruit of the Spirit is in all goodness and righteousness and truth;)
Proving what is acceptable unto the Lord." Ephesians 5:8-10

Therefore, as former citizens of Ethiopia are to continue to allow the *Gishon* to flow and encircle us until light is brought forth in all areas of our lives.

"And the name of the third river is Hiddekel: that is it which goeth toward the east of Assyria. And the fourth river is Euphrates." Genesis 2:14

The third river was **Hiddekel**, which means rapid. This river went toward the east of Assyria. Assyria means "a step" in the sense of being successful. The root meaning comes from the Hebrew word '*ashar* which means to go straight, advance, progress, to walk, or to righten. It is to pronounce happy or to be called blessed.

Hiddekel flowed in order to cause those to the east of Assyria to be upright and erect through the process of leading. Once we are whitened and brought forth into the light of God's presence we are to walk upright before him.

"The righteous shall flourish like the palm tree: he shall grow like a cedar in Lebanon." Psalm 92:12

"And I will bring the blind by a way that they knew not; I will lead them in paths that they have not known: I will make

darkness light before them, and crooked things straight. These things will I do unto them, and not forsake them."
Isaiah 42:16

The fourth river was **Euphrates**, which means fruitfulness. The Euphrates causes all to break forth with fruitfulness for the glory of God. In order to be fruitful we must be connected to the flow of God. We need to become one with his nature, essence, character, beliefs, and judgments. We must obey his commands and complete the process which he has laid out for us.

"Abide in me, and I in you. As the branch cannot bear fruit of itself, except it abide in the vine; no more can ye, except ye abide in me. I am the vine, ye are the branches: He that abideth in me, and I in him, the same bringeth forth much fruit: for without me ye can do nothing." John 15:4-5

If we refuse to abide in Christ, we will be barren. We will wither and eventually be discarded (John 15:6).

However, if we remain in him we can ask anything of him and it will be done for us (John 15:7).

As the branches of Christ, we will produce fruit against which there is no law.

"But the fruit of the Spirit is love, joy, peace, longsuffering, gentleness, goodness, faith, Meekness, temperance: against such there is no law." Galatians 5:22-23

Furthermore, we will please God, increase in the knowledge of God, and the work we do will be good and fruitful.

"That ye might walk worthy of the Lord unto all pleasing, being fruitful in every good work, and increasing in the knowledge of God;" Colossians 1:10

The flow of the God's word enables us to fulfil the original mandate of God to be fruitful, to multiply, subdue, exercise dominion, and replenish the earth.

"And God blessed them, and God said unto them, Be fruitful, and multiply, and replenish the earth, and subdue it: and have dominion over the fish of the sea, and over the fowl of the air, and over every living thing that moveth upon the earth." Genesis 1:28

In order to please God in the work he has assigned to us we need the combined flow of *Pison, Gihon, Hiddekel,* and *Euphrates* rivers in our lives. The river of God has the potential to make the inhabitants of the city of God glad. If we are willing to allow it to flow unhindered.

"There is a river, the streams whereof shall make glad the city of God, the holy place of the tabernacles of the most High." Psalm 46:4

The river of God flows from the throne of God and of the Lamb.

"And he shewed me a pure river of water of life, clear as crystal, proceeding out of

the throne of God and of the Lamb."
Revelation 22:1

If we allow God's word to ***rheō*** in our lives, all will know that we are his by the fruit we produce and the lives we live. We will be void of thorns and thistles. We will abandon our old nature and lay hold of a new one.

Ye shall know them by their fruits. Do men gather grapes of thorns, or figs of thistles?" Matthew 7:16

DAY 2

THE REVELATION OF GOD'S THOUGHTS

"For I know the thoughts that I think toward you, saith the LORD, thoughts of peace, and not of evil, to give you an expected end." Jeremiah 29:11

The expressed words of God are a revelation of his thoughts, plans, and judgments. They make known to man how he regards or considers things. They reveal how he devises and balances everything. Woven into the meaning of the word *thought* is the understanding that God's thoughts are calculated in order to invent all that should be to become.

It is for this reason that every word, which proceeds from the mouth of God, is to be considered and given weight. They are laden with power, life, life, and judgment.

According to Jeremiah 29:11, the Word of God reveals God's thoughts and plans for us. They are thoughts of peace and a future. The word used for **peace** is **shalowm** which means soundness, completeness, health, prosperity, friendship, safety, contentment, tranquility, and to safeguard our welfare.

God wants to pour favor on us; he desires to be our friend. He wants to give us good health and make us sound in every way. The peace he has for us is not the same, as the peace world gives.

"Peace I leave with you, my peace I give unto you: not as the world giveth, give I unto you. Let not your heart be troubled, neither let it be afraid." John 14:27

The peace that God offers is firm and stable, it is unshakeable and undeniable. It is pure, true, and good. Evil has no part of the peace of God. It is not malignant, unpleasant, displeasing, bad tempered or unkind nor is it wicked in any way. Misery and unhappiness is not found in the peace of God. It is not injurious or hurtful; it will not break our hearts or spirits. The peace of God does not cause injury. It is wholly good.

It is for this reason that God told Jeremiah that his thoughts of peace is without an evil component. Evil by its nature is destructive. It does not create a future. It does not prolong or give life. It shatters and breaks in pieces forcing an end. All that God does is with the purpose of continued life. God wants to give us a ground of hope, an expected outcome; he desires to fill us with expectation. God wants us to wait for it, to expect it, to look with great anticipation for the day. He wants us to linger or tarry for it with eagerness.

"For the vision is yet for an appointed time, but at the end it shall speak, and not lie: though it tarry, wait for it; because it will surely come, it will not tarry." Habakkuk 2:3

"Wait on the LORD: be of good courage, and he shall strengthen thine heart: wait, I say, on the LORD." Psalm 27:14

And, behold, I send the promise of my Father upon you: but tarry ye in the city of Jerusalem, until ye be endued with power from on high." Luke 24:49

"And, being assembled together with them, commanded them that they should not depart from Jerusalem, but wait for the promise of the Father, which, saith he, ye have heard of me." Acts 1:4

The thoughts of God are expressed though speech. If we adhere to the words of God they will accomplish in our lives what they were sent forth to do. There is unity or oneness between the thoughts of God and the Word of God that was manifested in the person of Jesus.

"For I have not spoken of myself; but the Father which sent me, he gave me a commandment, what I should say, and what I should speak." John 12:49

"Then said Jesus unto them, When ye have lifted up the Son of man, then shall ye know that I am he, and that I do nothing of myself; but as my Father hath taught me, I speak these things." John 8:28

Likewise, when we lift up the Word of God over our lives we join the oneness of God.

"If ye abide in me, and my words abide in you, ye shall ask what ye will, and it shall be done unto you." John 15:7

"That they all may be one; as thou, Father, art in me, and I in thee, that they also may be one in us: that the world may believe that thou hast sent me." John 17:21

This means that our words will no longer be our own. Our thoughts will not be independent or separate from the thoughts of God. In essence, we will have a like-mindedness, which comes from unification with the mind of Christ governed by the will of God.

The thoughts that God has towards us are innumerable. The Bible overflows with God's thoughts and plans toward us. Daily Holy Spirit reveals even more unto us. What we know is that when we hear the Word of God they are for life, hope, goodness, salvation, deliverance, protection, correction, healing, and for all that is righteous (2 Timothy 3:14-17).

"Many, O LORD my God, are thy wonderful works which thou hast done, and thy thoughts which are to us-ward: they cannot be reckoned up in order unto thee: if I would declare and speak of them, they are more than can be numbered." Psalms 40:5

Christ is the manifest expression of God's thoughts and intents therefore if we desire to understand and know God's thoughts toward us we must listen to the words spoken by Jesus.

"But he answered and said, It is written, Man shall not live by bread alone, but by every word that proceedeth out of the mouth of God." Matthew 4:4

DAY 3

GOD'S WORD IS A CASE OF LAW

The Word of God is a case at law. This legal term is defined according to BusinessDictionary.com as "Part of common law, consisting of judgments given by higher (appellate) courts in interpreting the statutes (or the provisions of a constitution) applicable in cases brought before them. Called precedents, they are binding on all courts (within the same jurisdiction) to be followed as the law in similar cases. Over time, these precedents are recognized, affirmed, and enforced by the subsequent court decisions, thus continually expanding the common law. In comparison, statute law is the body of acts enacted by a legislature, and civil law does not recognize any precedent."

The **rhēma** (Word) of God are judgments. They are the final and ultimate authority in any dispute. Although there appears to be an age-old disagreement between good and evil, between God and Satan there is only one Supreme Court with only one true judge, whose judgements set eternal precedent. These precedents are to be affirmed and enforced by the people of God daily as we live our lives.

Satan accuses us day and night (Revelation 12:10). He presents his arguments before the throne of God. He seeks to rob, kill, and destroy. He tries to oppose us and block us.

When we use the Word of God, we release a rebuke to Satan. The rebuke is a request for censure severely or an expression of formal disapproval. It is to charge sharply, reprove, chide, or merit a penalty. It is to request that he be taxed with fault against and before God. When we use the Word of God against Satan a fixed value is placed on his crime a debt that he will owe.

"And the LORD said unto Satan, The LORD rebuke thee, O Satan; even the LORD that hath chosen Jerusalem rebuke thee: is not this a brand plucked out of the fire?" Zechariah 3:2

"Yet Michael the archangel, when contending with the devil he disputed about the body of Moses, durst not bring against him a railing accusation, but said, The Lord rebuke thee." Jude 1:9

Satan rejected the Word of God and it is that same Word that will judge him. When we lift up the Word of God, it also adds charges to his account.

"He that rejecteth me, and receiveth not my words, hath one that judgeth him: the word that I have spoken, the same shall judge him in the last day." John 12:48

Jesus came to judge Satan and to destroy his works. Christ is the representative from the highest court. As representatives in the lower courts, we are to do as Christ did for the precedents that he established are binding for we are within the same jurisdiction as Christ.

"He that committeth sin is of the devil; for the devil sinneth from the beginning. For this purpose the Son of God was manifested, that he might destroy the works of the devil." 1 John 3:8

"Now is the judgment of this world: now shall the prince of this world be cast out." John 12:31

Christ overcame Satan and the world by the Word of God. Each word he spoke judged the world and stripped it of all pretense, deception, and illusion. Christ rendered it naked exposing its shame.

"These things I have spoken unto you, that in me ye might have peace. In the world ye shall have tribulation: but be of good cheer; I have overcome the world." John 16:33

In order to be overcomers we are to use the Word of God to judge what God has already judged. We are to use it to cast off the shame of the enemy. We are to allow it to cleanse us and declare the devil sinful for that is his nature from the beginning.

In each matter that is presented to us, we are to seek God's Word and uphold the case in law. We are to declare the legal rulings of God and our judicial decision are to be reflective of his.

DAY 4

GOD'S WORD IS A MESSAGE

The word *message* occurs seven times
in the King James Version of the Bible.
It is first used in Judges 3:20 when
Ehud went to the king of Moab and said
that he had a message for him from
God. *Ehud* was raised up by God as a
deliverer (Judges 3:15). The name *Ehud*
means, "I will give thanks: I will be
praised." He was a Benjamite judge
over Israel. The core meaning of Ehud
is undivided, union, or united.

When God raised up Ehud it was with
the intent of unifying the people with
himself.

"And he said unto them, Follow after me: for the LORD hath delivered your enemies the Moabites into your hand. And they went down after him, and took the fords of Jordan toward Moab, and suffered not a man to pass over." Judges 3:28

The people were unified and the land went undisturbed for eighty years (Judges 3:31), but when *Ehud* died the people once again did what was evil in the eyes of the Lord (Judges 4:1).

Ehud was used by God to send a message to both Moab and to Israel. For Moab, it was that God was a deliverer of his people. For Israel, it was that those who know their God they could do great exploits. Israel was made strong through their willing obedience to the ways of God. Union with God ushers in victory, safety, and protection.

Each word that is spoken by God is a message. They reveal his love as they shed light. As the people of God, we are to embrace the messages of God completely for they are life. His words are our strength and prepare the way before us even in the midst of our enemies. Our enemy exists in darkness, therefore when we use the Word of God we pierce darkness and expose all to the light of God.

"This then is the message which we have heard of him, and declare unto you, that God is light, and in him is no darkness at all." 1 John 1:5

Satan is full of hatred. His sole purpose is to rob, kill, and destroy (John 10:10) therefore, when we love we disarm him. We defeat him because life is always triumphant over death, and to love is the power of life.

"For this is the message that ye heard from the beginning, that we should love one another." 1 John 3:11

"And above all things have fervent charity among yourselves: for charity shall cover the multitude of sins." 1 Peter 4:8

DAY 5

THE WORD OF GOD IS HIS SPEECH TO MAN

"In the beginning was the Word, and the Word was with God, and the Word was God." John 1:1

Today, there are several public speakers many of whom make their living by motivating others. They are found in a multitude of fields and they span a host of categories. However, the chief public speaker the one of preeminence is Christ.

From ages past, he spoke the words of God. He declared the plan of God to the heavens and he established it in the stars. From eternity, Jesus has been the orator of God. When he came to earth in the flesh, he once again performed his duty and spoke forth the agenda and purpose of God.

Although Christ spoke to all men, only those who were of God heard the words of God.

"He that is of God heareth God's words: ye therefore hear them not, because ye are not of God." John 8:47

Currently many hear the words that Christ spoke and his words do not judge them because it is not the season for judgment. Rather it is the time of awareness and opportunity. God is giving men time to become aware of him. He has opened the door of opportunity unto them for salvation.

"And if any man hear my words, and believe not, I judge him not: for I came not to judge the world, but to save the world. John 12:47

However, on the last day, the same words of Christ that they ignored or rejected *will* indeed judge them. Those who fail to respond to the speech of Christ will have no defense, no argument, and no standing against the true witness of God (Revelation 3:14).

For the speech of God is infused without measure with the Spirit of God. Therefore, it is powerful, alive, and equipped with a voice.

"For he whom God hath sent speaketh the words of God: for God giveth not the Spirit by measure unto him." John 3:34

Every thought of God (Psalm 19:9), each word spoken by Christ (John 12:49) and related to us through Holy Spirit will be fulfilled (John 16:13). It is our responsibility to remember the words of God for they shall surely come to pass.

"Saying, The Son of man must be delivered into the hands of sinful men, and be crucified, and the third day rise again. And they remembered his words, And returned from the sepulchre, and told all these things unto the eleven, and to all the rest." Luke 24:7-9

As it was in past times so shall it be in future times!

"For God hath put in their hearts to fulfil his will, and to agree, and give their kingdom unto the beast, until the words of God shall be fulfilled." Revelation 17:17

"Hear ye the word which the LORD speaketh unto you, O house of Israel:" Jeremiah 10:1

"And he said unto them, He that hath ears to hear, let him hear." Mark 4:9

"Heaven and earth shall pass away, but my words shall not pass away." Matthew 24:35

DAY 6

THE DISCOURSE OF GOD'S WORD

"And the LORD said, Shall I hide from Abraham that thing which I do; Seeing that Abraham shall surely become a great and mighty nation, and all the nations of the earth shall be blessed in him?" Genesis 18:17-18

In the Bible, we are given several examples of deliberation between God and his servants. One such discourse occurred between Abraham and the Lord over what was to occur in Sodom and Gomorrah (Genesis 18).

In Exodus 3, the angel of the Lord appeared unto Moses and spoke the thoughts and intents of God to Moses. Moses was engaged in a supernatural communication and he was given an opportunity to respond to what he heard. In verse 11, Moses questioned God. In verse 13, he asked how to answer their inevitable questions. In Exodus 4:1, Moses revealed to God his belief that the people would not hearken unto his voice nor would they believe him. By verse 10, Moses revealed what he believed to be true about himself that he was not an eloquent speaker and he possessed a slow tongue. In verse 13, Moses asked God to send someone else on the challenging mission.

In Exodus 32, the Lord had another discussion with Moses in which he told him that he would make a great nation of him. Moses heard the word of the Lord, yet he was compelled to reason with God. Moses reminded God of his promises to Abraham, Isaac, and Israel. Moses pointed out that the Egyptians would speak wickedly about him. They would tarnish his good reputation.

In 1 Kings 19 the Lord spoke with Elijah and Elijah spoke to the Lord. They engaged in discourse. The word discourse means to debate, to discuss, to have a conference, or a consultation. In each situation, we see that when the Word of the Lord came the servant of God had an opportunity to speak freely with God.

In Judges 6:12, the angel of the Lord appeared to Gideon. In verse 13, Gideon questioned the Lord's messenger.

"And Gideon said unto him, Oh my Lord, if the LORD be with us, why then is all this befallen us? and where be all his miracles which our fathers told us of, saying, Did not the LORD bring us up from Egypt? but now the LORD hath forsaken us, and delivered us into the hands of the Midianites." Judges 6:13

The Word of God is sent to engage us. It opens the door of reasoning and paves the way for understanding. When the Lord releases his Word it reveals the mind and heart of God and lifts us to a higher place of understanding.

"Come now, and let us reason together, saith the LORD: though your sins be as scarlet, they shall be as white as snow; though they be red like crimson, they shall be as wool." Isaiah 1:18

Although God's Word is perfect, pure, and true it matters to him that we have understanding. He desires for us to understand the nature and purpose of his Word. God's Word comes to reveal who we were created to be as seen in the lives of Moses and Gideon. His Word reveals his intent and to cause us to respond with hearts of compassion and sound judgment as seen with Abraham and Moses. God's Word comes to correct us and to turn us from abandoning the call that has been placed on our lives as in the case of Elijah.

No matter the purpose for which God's Word is sent, there is an opportunity for the servant of God to ask, question, express, and to reason with him. However, it is the prerogative of God to decide how he will respond to our inquiries or statements.

DAY 7

GOD'S WORD IS A LAMP UNTO MY FEET

"NUN. Thy word is a lamp unto my feet, and a light unto my path." Psalm 119:105

The sayings and promises of God are a *lamp* unto the feet of his people. The Hebrew word *niyr* is used for the word lamp. It means to break up, till, or fleshly plough. It has a root meaning of fire or fiery. It means to shine or to glisten. Woven into the meaning of the word lamp is the notion of a fresh furrow.

A *furrow* is a long trench that is used for the planting of seeds. Therefore, the word *lamp* in Psalm 119:105 reveals to us the purpose of the Word of God. God's word is to break up tough ground within us. It is to dig a trench into which the seeds of life can be planted and deeply rooted.

"Hear ye therefore the parable of the sower. When any one heareth the word of the kingdom, and understandeth it not, then cometh the wicked one, and catcheth away that which was sown in his heart. This is he which received seed by the way side. But he that received the seed into stony places, the same is he that heareth the word, and anon with joy receiveth it; Yet hath he not root in himself, but dureth for a while: for when tribulation or persecution ariseth because of the word, by and by he is offended. He also that received seed among the thorns is he that heareth the word; and the care of this world, and the deceitfulness of riches, choke the word, and he becometh unfruitful. But he that received seed into the good ground is he that heareth the word, and understandeth it; which also beareth fruit, and bringeth forth, some an hundredfold, some sixty, some thirty."
Matthew 13:18-23

Hence, the Word of God has a job to perform which if permitted will produce fruitfulness in the lives of all who use it as light. The Word of God is also a trying fire. It refines us as an artisan removing dross from the top of molten metal.

"For other foundation can no man lay than that is laid, which is Jesus Christ. Now if any man build upon this foundation gold, silver, precious stones, wood, hay, stubble; Every man's work shall be made manifest: for the day shall declare it, because it shall be revealed by fire; and the fire shall try every man's work of what sort it is. If any man's work abide which he hath built thereupon, he shall receive a reward. If any man's work shall be burned, he shall suffer loss: but he himself shall be saved; yet so as by fire." 1 Corinthians 3:11-15

The purpose of the Word of God is to duplicate the character and nature of God in the sons of God. The process nears completion when the fruit of the Spirit is produced in our lives with consistency.

The influence of the lamp of God is evidenced in the way we walk, proceed, explore and speak of others. Do we insult others? Are we news carriers? How do we view others, situations, or the world? What motivates us as we advance in life?

It is the Word of God that will enable us to advance with spiritual prosperity. It is the declarations of God that will help us to walk along a straight path. It is his Word that will "righten" us as we go forward in life. This opens the way for us to do as Christ has done. Christ came he ploughed and he watered and God has given the increase.

"Verily, verily, I say unto you, He that believeth on me, the works that I do shall he do also; and greater works than these shall he do; because I go unto my Father." John 14:12

"I have planted, Apollos watered; but God gave the increase." 1 Corinthians 3:6

The day is coming when each will receive his own reward. If we allow the Word of God to complete its work then our reward will be grand to the glory of God.

"Now he that planteth and he that watereth are one: and every man shall receive his own reward according to his own labour." 1 Corinthians 3:8

DAY 8

GOD'S WORD IS LIGHT AND BRIGHTNESS

"The people which sat in darkness saw great light; and to them which sat in the region and shadow of death light is sprung up." Matthew 4:16

There are many facets to the Word of God! For those who live in darkness it is a bright light that shines forth beckoning them to come. It is this aspect of the word of God that we will highlight. In order to grasp the significance of the brightness of God's Word let us look at the words of the prophet Isaiah.

"Nevertheless the dimness shall not be such as was in her vexation, when at the first he lightly afflicted the land of Zebulun and the land of Naphtali, and afterward did more grievously afflict her

*by the way of the sea, beyond Jordan, in
Galilee of the nations. The people that
walked in darkness have seen a great
light: they that dwell in the land of the
shadow of death, upon them hath the
light shined." Isaiah 9:1-2*

Isaiah spoke these words to the
children of Israel who refused to hear
or receive the word that the Lord sent
for them (Isaiah 8:6). They decided
that they would believe *only* the words
that pleased them. They focused on
the aspect of God that delighted them.
They stood firm in the notion that
Jehovah would protect them in spite of
their waywardness.

Because of their refusal, God punished
them. He allowed their enemy to come
and afflict them. God allowed them to
pursue their course into deeper realms
of darkness. However, God gave them
a promise that *light* would come again
to those who walked in darkness. This
word was God's assurance that an
opportunity would be given in the
future.

Matthew 4:12-16, chronicles the fulfillment of the words of Isaiah. Jesus the *bright light* of God went to the land of the shadow of death and shined. The inhabitants of the land were given an opportunity to receive light. An invitation was extended to them to walk in the true light of God.

The Word of God was sent to the land of **Zabulon**. The Hebrew word for *Zabulon* is **Zaboulōn** and it means a habitation. As we study its root meaning, we learn that it refers to being exalted, honored, and dwelling in an exalted manner. The Gesenius' Hebrew-Chaldee Lexicon states it means to be round or to make round as in the dung of camels or goats. It is to dwell together in a conjoined manner. Therefore, the people were as compact waste. They were joined together in an intimate bond. They thought highly of themselves. Yet they lived in pure darkness and they were living lives that were of no benefit to the *spiritual* body of God. The inhabitants of *Zabulon* were ignorant of their true state.

The Word of God was sent to the land of **Nephthalim**. *Nephthalim* derives its meaning from the Hebrew word **Naphtaliy (Naphtali)** the word for **wrestling**. The root word for *Naphtaliy* comes from **Pathal (Niphal)** which means to be twisted, deceitful, crafty, or to act perversely. **Niphal** reveals the character and nature of the inhabitants of *Nephthalim*. The original use of the word **Naphtali** is found in Genesis 30:8.

"And Rachel said, With great wrestlings have I wrestled with my sister, and I have prevailed: and she called his name Naphtali." Genesis 30:8

In Genesis 30:8, Rachel speaks of contending with her sister. The *wrestling (naphtuwl)* she had to go through. The fact that she *wrestled (pathal)* and prevailed. How did she prevail? She was crafty with a touch of deceit. The people of the land of Nephthalim possessed Rachel's craftiness. They wrestled to get what they wanted and used cunning to their advantage. From this, we can deduce that prevailing over others was important to the inhabitants of the land of Nephthalim for it was important to the mother who named Naphtali.

Jesus the Word of God was sent to visit those who had descended or sank down from a position of true honor in God. He traveled along the path of the river to the other side of Jordan. The word *beyond* means on the other side. However, its meaning goes deeper for it means to pierce. When Christ went *beyond* the Jordan, he *pierced* through the darkness that engulfed the people giving them an opportunity to receive light.

Jordan means "the descender." It means to come down, sink down, decline, to march down or to go down. It also means to come down in terms of revelation. The inhabitants of the land had come down to such a state that they no longer had the revelation of God. They were engulfed in darkness devoid of light. Their refusal to heed the words of God had brought them low in spiritual matters. Christ went down in order to lift them up to their rightful position.

The *Gentiles* had become accustom to darkness. Yet God decided it was time for them to have an opportunity to enter into the light. The core meaning for *Galilee* is to roll way or to roll as in stones, to roll down. It is a turning or a folding. Jesus went to Galilee to roll away stones from their graves. He went there to open the door of life unto them. He folded it back so that their insides could receive the brightness of day light. He brought with him the hope of new life.

When the Word of God comes into the life of a person it provides an opportunity for brightness, an opportunity to abandon what one was accustom to, it opens sepulchers, and it swings open doors. It releases captives and pierces the eyes of those surrounded by darkness.

What has the Word of God done for you? Are you willing to allow Jesus to pierce through all darkness in your life? Are you willing to let him swing open prison doors for you? Are you willing to receive the Word that God sent for you? The Word of *spiritual* revelation? The Word that will elevate you to your rightful position in the family of God?

DAY 9

GOD'S WORD IS SPIRITUAL UNDERSTANDING

"And I have filled him with the spirit of God, in wisdom, and in understanding, and in knowledge, and in all manner of workmanship," Exodus 31:3

The word **understanding** (**tabuwn**) was first used in Exodus 31:3. God used this word when he informed Moses that he had called Bezaleel the son of Uri the son of Hur by name. The Lord told Moses that Bezaleel had been filled with the spirit of God in wisdom, knowledge, and understanding. The word of God fashioned Bezaleel for the task that lay ahead of him.

In order to grasp what Bezaleel was fashioned with we must look closely at the Hebrew word for *understanding tabuwn*. **Tabuwn** is to have skill, intelligence, knowledge. It is to discern, perceive, and possess insight. It is to be prudent, with the ability to teach and instruct. The core meaning of *understanding* possessing the ability to distinguish one thing from another. It is the ability to separate things so that they stand apart (separately). *Understanding* is considering a matter and having the skill to explain it or declare what it is.

God fashioned Bezaleel with the comprehensive nature of understanding so that he could accomplish the task that was assigned to him. Why did God choose Bezaleel?

Bezaleel's name means in the shadow of God or under the protection of God. Could it be that Bezaleel lived a life that bore out his name?

"He that dwelleth in the secret place of the most High shall abide under the shadow of the Almighty." Psalms 91:1

Bezaleel was the son of *Uri*. *Uri's* name means fiery, light of fire, flame. Its root means to be illuminated, to become light, or to shine. Therefore, Bezaleel was trained by his father to be light, to shine, and to be hot for God. His father Uri was the son of *Hur*. The root meaning of the name *Hur* is to be white, to grow white or white cloth. The literal meaning of *Hur* is "hole" as in the dwelling place of a snake (Isaiah 11:8). This reveals that a process of transformation occurred in the life of Hur for he moved from being in a dark place to a place that enabled him to grow white. He moved from the under the influence of one entity darkness into the domain of another light. By the time Uri was born, the light had gotten brighter and hotter for the Lord. When Bezaleel arrived, his habitation was no longer in a "hole" but under the shadow of the almighty. In essence, he dwelt in the presence of light.

The Word of the Lord prepared Bezaleel in the way of understanding and it is the same opportunity God's Word provides for us today.

"That the God of our Lord Jesus Christ, the Father of glory, may give unto you the spirit of wisdom and revelation in the knowledge of him:" Ephesians 1:17

"But the natural man receiveth not the things of the Spirit of God: for they are foolishness unto him: neither can he know them, because they are spiritually discerned." 1 Corinthians 2:14

"It is the spirit that quickeneth; the flesh profiteth nothing: the words that I speak unto you, they are spirit, and they are life." John 6:63

Paul discerned the value of the Word of God. He prayed that God would give it unto us the same way Jehovah provided it for Bezaleel. The revelation in the knowledge of God means that God would make things naked before us. He would disclose truth and instruction unto us. Paul asked that

God would reveal things that were formally unknown. Why was it important to Paul that God remove the veil?

Paul understood that with revelation we would be equipped with understanding. We would be able to distinguish good from evil, righteousness from unrighteousness, darkness from light, and ascending from descending. The truth is only God can give us the correct and precise knowledge of himself. Only God truly knows himself therefore, he would have to reveal to us who he is, what he desires, and what he intends.

Bezaleel was charged with the duty of devising cunning works in gold, silver, and brass. He had to cut stones and set them. He was responsible for carving timber in all manner of workmanship (service, work, or use). He was a messenger of God for this purpose according to the root meaning of workmanship. Likewise, we are messengers of God and in order for us to fulfill our purpose; we need to be filled with the spirit of God. God's Word is spirit therefore; we need to be filled with his Word, in the name of Jesus.

DAY 10

GOD'S WORD BUILDS EXCELLENCE OF CHARACTER

"Then this Daniel was preferred above the presidents and princes, because an excellent spirit was in him; and the king thought to set him over the whole realm." Daniel 6:3

The Word of God establishes excellence of character. This fact is demonstrated in the life of Daniel. Although the Bible does not catalog when God called Daniel, it does chronical his faithfulness to God and his excellence of character. In order to understand how Daniel achieved excellence of character we need to examine his name.

Daniel means God is my judge. It gets its root meaning from two Hebrew words **Dan** which means a judge and *'el* which means god-like one, mighty one, or mighty hero. Let us look at the core of each word so we can discover what caused Daniel to live a life of excellence before God and men.

The word *Dan* gets its meaning from the Hebrew word ***diyn*** and ***'adown***. *Diyn* means to plead, contend, judge, govern, plead a cause, vindicate, and to execute judgment. When we examine Daniels life, we see that Daniel judged matters. He chose not to defile himself (Daniel 1:8). In Daniel 6:10, he judged the decree of men less important than serving God faithfully. Daniel had a position of governance in Babylon (Daniel 2:49). Daniel was vindicated by God for Jehovah protected him in the lion's den (Daniel 6:19-24). Therefore, it is clear that Daniel lived up to the meaning of Dan for he judged matters well in the eyes of the Lord.

The word *'adown* means firm, master, lord, strong. Its base meaning is to rule. This indicates that Daniel ruled with strength and from a firm foundation. That foundation was the word of God. Because he studied the word and continually sought the will of God Daniel's character was one of excellence.

The Hebrew word *'el* is the one that is used for Jesus in the Bible. It describes the nature and character of the son of God. Daniel had the character of the Son of God. He was a god-like one, a mighty man, one who served the one true God. The base meaning of *'el* comes from the Hebrew words *'ayil* and **'uwl**. *'Ayil* means ram. It represents the ram that is used for food, as a sacrifice, tabernacle, and as a red dye. It also represents a doorpost, strong man, leader, and chief. **'Uwl** means to twist, prominence, to be strong.

From this, we see that Daniel had the nature of Christ. He was a mighty one. He served only God. He possessed understanding for he was able to distinguish what was right and pleasing to God and what was not. He led people through his sound judgments (Daniel 6:26). By standing firm in the ways of God Daniel demonstrated strength and character. He went into the lion's den as a lamb, yet he came out as a conquering lion.

"I have even heard of thee, that the spirit of the gods is in thee, and that light and understanding and excellent wisdom is found in thee." Daniel 5:14

"Forasmuch as an excellent spirit, and knowledge, and understanding, interpreting of dreams, and shewing of hard sentences, and dissolving of doubts, were found in the same Daniel, whom the king named Belteshazzar: now let Daniel be called, and he will shew the interpretation." Daniel 5:12

The Word of God spoken over our lives is mighty and powerful. It develops the spirit of excellence in us for it is rooted in *pure truth.*

"Sanctify them through thy truth: thy word is truth." John 17:17

If we allow God's Word to complete its duty in our lives, we will be established in righteousness. It will make our judgements sound and pleasing unto god.

"Thy word is true from the beginning: and every one of thy righteous judgments endureth for ever." Psalms 119:160

God's Word provides understanding which testifies of an excellent spirit.

"He that hath knowledge spareth his words: and a man of understanding is of an excellent spirit." Proverbs 17:27

The Aramaic word **yattiyr** is used in Daniel 5:12 and 5:14 for the word **excellent**. It means pre-eminent, extreme, extraordinary, and surpassing. It is to show excess or to have left over. In essence, it is to have abundance. Daniel had a wealth of excellent of character.

The Hebrew word **yaqar** is used for **excellent** in Proverbs 17:27. It means to be weighty, rare, precious, highly valued, as in precious stones or jewels. Its root meaning is to be esteemed, to be costly, appraised, or highly valued. When we receive the Word of God, the spirit of excellence we become a rarity, we become highly valued, we become as precious stones.

"To whom coming, as unto a living stone, disallowed indeed of men, but chosen of God, and precious, Ye also, as lively stones, are built up a spiritual house, an holy priesthood, to offer up spiritual sacrifices, acceptable to God by Jesus Christ. Wherefore also it is contained in the scripture, Behold, I lay in Sion a chief corner stone, elect, precious: and he that believeth on him shall not be confounded. Unto you therefore which believe he is precious: but unto them which be disobedient, the stone which the builders disallowed, the same is made the head of the corner, And a stone of stumbling, and a rock of offence, even to them which stumble at the word, being disobedient: whereunto also they were appointed. But ye are a chosen generation, a royal priesthood, an holy nation, a peculiar people; that ye should shew forth the praises of him who hath called you out of darkness into his

marvellous light: Which in time past were not a people, but are now the people of God: which had not obtained mercy, but now have obtained mercy." 1 Peter 2:4-10

DAY 11

GOD'S WORD IS FOOD FOR GROWTH

"Give us this day our daily bread."
Matthew 6:11

God sent Jesus on a mission to the earth. It was a mission that had many dimensions to it. Christ came to save, deliver, and set fallen men free. He came to offer us a way to be reconciled to God. He also came to destroy the works of the enemy as he argued the case of God before all. Christ was God's legal advocate for he presented the *true* picture of God. He revealed to us what was hidden. As wonderful as this is Christ did more. He became food unto us. He was and is the bread of life. He is the food for the mighty. He is the spiritual meat that enables us to grow in the ways of God.

"Man did eat angels' food: he sent them meat to the full." Psalm 78:25

Similar to the manna that fell from heaven, Christ is available for our daily nutrition. When we find the words of God we are to consume them for they will bring joy and rejoicing to our hearts.

"Thy words were found, and I did eat them; and thy word was unto me the joy and rejoicing of mine heart: for I am called by thy name, O LORD God of hosts." Jeremiah 15:16

If we receive them with the right attitude, we will learn to value them more than natural food. In order for us to live as sons of God, we have to feast on the food supplied by God (Matthew 4:4). Christ depended on every word that the Father gave him.

"Neither have I gone back from the commandment of his lips; I have esteemed the words of his mouth more than my necessary food." Job 23:12

At times, the word that we receive from Jehovah may be bitter. It may offend our sensibilities. It may cause our flesh to scream in rebellion, but if we continue to eat it trusting God it will become sweet unto us.

"And I went unto the angel, and said unto him, Give me the little book. And he said unto me, Take it, and eat it up; and it shall make thy belly bitter, but it shall be in thy mouth sweet as honey."
Revelation 10:9

God's word may reveal things that are awful and terrible, but it is always sweet to obey the will and purpose of God. In Acts 9:16, the Lord revealed to Ananias that Paul would have to suffer many things in the name of Jesus (Acts 22:11-15).

Paul understood from the beginning the task for which he was called. In 2 Corinthians 11:16-33, Paul lists all that he suffered for Jesus. It was bitter yet he counted it all joy (2 Corinthians 12:10, Acts 21:11-14). Paul was pleased that he did not turn away from the ways of God. He completed the race and he put up a good fight. He was confident that a crown of righteousness awaited him (1 Timothy 4:7-8). Paul chose consume the sweet words of God.

"How sweet are thy words unto my taste! yea, sweeter than honey to my mouth!" Psalms 119:103

He opted to grow unto perfection.

"Therefore leaving the principles of the doctrine of Christ, let us go on unto perfection; not laying again the foundation of repentance from dead works, and of faith toward God," Hebrews 6:1

He decided not to follow the ways of the rebellious.

"But thou, son of man, hear what I say unto thee; Be not thou rebellious like that rebellious house: open thy mouth, and eat that I give thee." Ezekiel 2:8

He was not finicky about what God placed before him. Whatever he was given, he ate.

"And he said unto me, Son of man, cause thy belly to eat, and fill thy bowels with this roll that I give thee. Then did I eat it; and it was in my mouth as honey for sweetness." Ezekiel 3:3

He understood that it was God's right and duty to give food to him.

"Who giveth food to all flesh: for his mercy endureth for ever." Psalm 136:25

"Which executeth judgment for the oppressed: which giveth food to the hungry. The LORD looseth the prisoners:" Psalm 146:7

"Nevertheless he left not himself without witness, in that he did good, and gave us rain from heaven, and fruitful seasons, filling our hearts with food and gladness." Acts 14:17

"Now he that ministereth seed to the sower both minister bread for your food,

*and multiply your seed sown, and
increase the fruits of your
righteousness;)" 2 Corinthians 9:10*

Our *spiritual* growth is dependent on
one thing. Are we willing to eat the
food of the mighty? Are we willing to
consume the meal that Jehovah has
provided? Are we going to feast on the
bread of life completely? If we refuse
to eat, what God has provided we will
not grow with strength or power!

We will be like the children of Israel
who despised the *light bread* of God.

*"And the people spake against God, and
against Moses, Wherefore have ye
brought us up out of Egypt to die in the
wilderness? for there is no bread, neither
is there any water; and our soul loatheth
this light bread." Numbers 21:5*

They tested God and he responded
(Numbers 21:6).

*"Neither let us tempt Christ, as some of
them also tempted, and were destroyed
of serpents." 1 Corinthians 10:9*

Jehovah is a good God. Let us trust him in all things knowing that his food is beneficial for our *spiritual growth*.

DAY 12

GOD'S WORD PIERCES THE EYES

"The light of the body is the eye: if therefore thine eye be single, thy whole body shall be full of light." Matthew 6:22

In Matthew 6:22, God reveals that the eye is the light of the body. What does this phrase mean? The Greek word **lychnos** is used for light. It refers to a candle, lamp, or candlestick. It gets its core meaning from the word **leukos** which means brilliant, bright, dazzling white or dead white light. The type of light referenced here is as the garments of angels or of those robed in splendor and of heavenly state. It is a light that goes beyond signifying purity and innocence of the soul. It is this type of light that is useful to the body.

Why does the body need light? **Sōma** is the word used for body. It means the body of an animal, men, or a corpse. *Sōma* gets its root meaning from the word **sōzō**, which means to rescue from destruction or danger, to keep safe, sound, or to save from injury or peril.

Therefore, the dazzling white light full of heavenly splendor keeps the body safe. It protects it from danger and safeguards it from destruction. Jesus is the great light that came to save us from injury and peril.

"Then spake Jesus again unto them, saying, I am the light of the world: he that followeth me shall not walk in darkness, but shall have the light of life." John 8:12

As the manifested Word of God, Jesus came to pierce our eyes with the dazzling light of God. Why?

In Matthew 6:22, we are given an inkling of what occurred. Light came into the body to save it. It affects our eyes transforming it in a sense. Although we have two eyes, the verse uses the singular tense. This indicates that our eyes merge and become one. That is why the word *if* is used. This transformation process is optional. The word **haplous** is used for single. It means to be whole, simple, sound, or when good fulfills its office. The core meaning comes from the words **plekō** and **alpha. Plekō** means union, to weave together, to plait or braid. **Alpha** represents the first letter of the Greek alphabet. It is also used to refer to Christ in terms of him being the first or the beginning.

"And if one prevail against him, two shall withstand him; and a threefold cord is not quickly broken." Ecclesiastes 4:12

"I am Alpha and Omega, the beginning and the end, the first and the last." Revelation 22:13

Therefore, the *union* that takes place when we allow light to transform our eyes plaits us together with Christ

(Colossians 1:12). This union causes our bodies to be full of light for we become one with the first of all things—Christ.

"Who is the image of the invisible God, the firstborn of every creature: For by him were all things created, that are in heaven, and that are in earth, visible and invisible, whether they be thrones, or dominions, or principalities, or powers: all things were created by him, and for him: And he is before all things, and by him all things consist. And he is the head of the body, the church: who is the beginning, the firstborn from the dead; that in all things he might have the preeminence. For it pleased the Father that in him should all fullness dwell; And, having made peace through the blood of his cross, by him to reconcile all things unto himself; by him, I say, whether they be things in earth, or things in heaven." Colossians 1:15-20

Christ was and is the first Word of God (John 1:1). He was the first of God's creation (Colossians 1:15), in safety (Proverbs 18:10, John 5:19, John 12:49,

Proverbs 7:1, Proverbs 22:18), in light, in prosperity, obedience (Hebrews 5:8), righteousness (1 Corinthians 1:30), life (John 11:25), unification (John 10:30), and in purity (1 John 3:3).

The apostle Paul underwent a similar transformation, as must we.

"And it came to pass, that, as I made my journey, and was come nigh unto Damascus about noon, suddenly there shone from heaven a great light round about me." Acts 22:6

"And when I could not see for the glory of that light, being led by the hand of them that were with me, I came into Damascus." Acts 22:11

"Then Paul answered, What mean ye to weep and to break mine heart? for I am ready not to be bound only, but also to die at Jerusalem for the name of the Lord Jesus." Acts 21:13

Paul was unified with Christ. He was willing to walk the path that Jesus walked to the point of death.
"He that saith he abideth in him ought himself also so to walk, even as he walked." 1 John 2:6

When the light of Christ pierces our eyes, we will desire to keep his commandments. We will have a singleness of focus. Our eyes will operate as a unit to safeguard the body, dispelling darkness, and ushering in more securely the light of Christ. To be dazzling brilliance is our duty. We are to pursue it until his appearing.

"Again, a new commandment I write unto you, which thing is true in him and in you: because the darkness is past, and the true light now shineth." 1 John 2:8

"Beloved, now are we the sons of God, and it doth not yet appear what we shall be: but we know that, when he shall appear, we shall be like him; for we shall see him as he is." 1 John 3:2

DAY 13

GOD'S WORD IS FOR REPROOF

"All scripture is given by inspiration of God, and is profitable for doctrine, for reproof, for correction, for instruction in righteousness: That the man of God may be perfect, thoroughly furnished unto all good works." 2 Timothy 3:16-17

The word of God is good for reproof! It is proven, tested, and sure. It is able to bring conviction to the soul and it can stand on its own against every argument. The Greek word **elegchos** is used for the word reproof. It means proof by a thing that has been tested and proven. *Elegchos* gets its core meaning from **elegchō** that means to convict correct, refute, expose, or to bring to light.

Hidden within the word *elegchō* are the means by which correction can take place. The word of God is not limited in its scope or power. It can address the heart of man through confutation. This is done by showing the person that the course along which they are traversing will result in shame.

God's word also convicts when it exposes the lost to the light of Christ (John 3:20, John 12:32).

"But all things that are reproved are made manifest by the light: for whatsoever doth make manifest is light." Ephesians 5:13

God's word can also chide a person. God can call us to give an account of something that we have done. He can demand an explanation.

"So then every one of us shall give account of himself to God." Romans 14:12

"For we must all appear before the judgment seat of Christ; that every one may receive the things done in his body,

according to that he hath done, whether it be good or bad." 2 Corinthians 5:10

"But I say unto you, That every idle word that men shall speak, they shall give account thereof in the day of judgment." Matthew 12:36

God's Word can also correct by deed. It is able to punish us(1 Timothy 5:20).

"Remember therefore from whence thou art fallen, and repent, and do the first works; or else I will come unto thee quickly, and will remove thy candlestick out of his place, except thou repent." Revelation 2:5

"As many as I love, I rebuke and chasten: be zealous therefore, and repent." Revelation 3:19

DAY 14

GOD'S WORD IS FOR CORRECTION

"All scripture is given by inspiration of God, and is profitable for doctrine, for reproof, for correction, for instruction in righteousness: That the man of God may be perfect, thoroughly furnished unto all good works." 2 Timothy 3:16-17

In 2 Timothy 3, Paul tells us that the word of God is profitable for correction. What did he mean? What is correction? How can the word of God help? What does it mean to be profitable?

Profitable (ophelos) is defined as benefitting, accumulating something for an advantage; it is to heap up like in a mound or a substantial portion. Therefore, Paul is telling us that if we accumulate the Word of God within ourselves it will be to our benefit.

The Word of God is needful to our spiritual progression for it restores us to an upright state. It prevents us from becoming bent, twisted, or spiritually deformed. It improves our character and our lives. God has made a way through his word to transform us from deformed individuals into erect people. His word is what builds us anew.

The Bibles tells of a woman who was disabled by a spirit for 18 years. One Sabbath, she encountered the Word of God. The representative of God told her that she was set free. He touched her and she immediately straightened up.

"And he laid his hands on her: and immediately she was made straight, and glorified God." Luke 13:13

"Wherefore lift up the hands which hang down, and the feeble knees; And make straight paths for your feet, lest that which is lame be turned out of the way; but let it rather be healed." Hebrews 12:12-13

The fact that Christ healed her on the Sabbath day speaks volumes. The Sabbath represented rest, the ceasing of weekly or ordinary activities. It meant putting an end to something, exterminating a thing, or causing a thing to fail.

Jesus, the Word of God, laid hands on her that brought about the immediate manifestation of healing. The deformity in her body and character was corrected. The spirit of disability was exterminated. Christ caused it to fail. The foul spirit had to desist from its work within the woman's body.

The Greek word **epitithēmi** was used for **laid**. It represents and active voice. It means to throw one's self upon something, to attack someone or to assault something. It is to lay aside, to bend down, or to establish as in ordain a thing. From this, we see that when Christ laid his hand on the woman he was firmly fixing the Word he had spoken over her. He was assaulting the thing that was inflicting disability upon her. When Jesus placed his hands on her, he bridged the gap between sickness and healing. He was the channel through which the power of God established her wellness (*chasma*). Jesus came to the woman's aid and he protected her from further harm. He established his right to determine and control her destiny (*cheir*).

Jesus restored the woman to an erect state like a palm tree. The distinguishing characteristic of a palm tree is that it grows erect (Songs of Solomon 7:7). The word of God comes to raise us up by restoring our strength.

"The righteous shall flourish like the palm tree: he shall grow like a cedar in Lebanon. Those that be planted in the house of the LORD shall flourish in the courts of our God. They shall still bring

forth fruit in old age; they shall be fat and flourishing; To shew that the LORD is upright: he is my rock, and there is no unrighteousness in him." Psalm 92:12-15

When we allow the word of God to correct us, it will cause us to flourish in the courts of God as it causes us to bring forth fruit even in old age. Furthermore, it testifies that the Lord is upright and full of righteousness. What is evident is that not only does the Word of God correct defects in our character, deformities in our bodies; it also established the correct order of things in God's creation. The disabling spirit was never meant to dwell in the woman's body. Therefore, Jesus established the righteous order of things.

DAY 15

GOD'S WORD IS FOR INSTRUCTION IN RIGHTEOUSNESS

"All scripture is given by inspiration of God, and is profitable for doctrine, for reproof, for correction, for instruction in righteousness: That the man of God may be perfect, thoroughly furnished unto all good works." 2 Timothy 3:16-17

What does it mean to be *instructed* in righteousness? The Greek word **paideia** was used to explain **instruction**. It is the educating of and the complete training of children. It is the cultivation of the mind, morals, soul, and the care of the body. It includes all the ways that children are taught. It includes physical punishment, words of correction, and through admonitions (counsel or warnings). In essence, the Word of God trains God's children in the way they are to go.

"Train up a child in the way he should go: and when he is old, he will not depart from it." Proverbs 22:6

Not everyone who professes to be a child of God is! A child is one who is subject to the authority of God as a slave is to a master or as a servant to the lord of the house.

When we receive the Word of God, our lessons begin. We begin to learn how to attain a "state of approval" by God. God's Word trains us in integrity, purity, virtue, how to act, and the proper way to think, respond, and feel about things. We learn to value and treasure divine laws. Gods' Word takes us into more difficult or challenging truths. If we prefer to remain in the simple and less controversial truths of God, we doom ourselves to being unskillful babes.

"For every one that useth milk is unskilful in the word of righteousness: for he is a babe." Hebrews 5:13

God is not grooming us to be stunted children. He desires to have mature children after the pattern of Jesus. We are to eat **strong** meat. The strength of our meat signifies the firmness of the Word that we digest. Strong meat will make us firm, hard, immovable, and steadfast. It will cause us to stand.

"But strong meat belongeth to them that are of full age, even those who by reason of use have their senses exercised to discern both good and evil." Hebrews 5:14

"Wherefore take unto you the whole armour of God, that ye may be able to withstand in the evil day, and having done all, to stand." Ephesians 6:13

The Word of God will prevent us from wavering. We will not hesitate to follow the will of God. His Word will make us like a fortified building built on the foundation of Christ.

"Thy righteousness is an everlasting righteousness, and thy law is the truth." Psalm 119:142

"Thy word is true from the beginning: and every one of thy righteous judgments endureth for ever." Psalm 119:160

God's Word is eternally righteous therefore; it is able to instruct us in righteousness. Furthermore, whenever he acts or judges a case it is righteous therefore it is sound and immovable. God desires that we reflect his nature that is why he sent his Word to instruct and teach us the ways of righteousness.

DAY 16

GOD'S WORD SANCTIFIES

"Sanctify them through thy truth: thy word is truth." John 17:17

The word *sanctify* appears in both the Old and the New Testament. The Hebrew word for **sanctify** is **qadash** and the Greek is **hagiazō**. *Qadash* means to be separate, hallowed, to observe as holy, to consecrate or to dedicate. In reference to God it is to cause himself to be hallowed to keep himself set apart, or to be observed as holy.

Hagiazō means to dedicate or consecrate things or people to God, to purify, cleanse internally and externally, to separate from profane things, or to be renewed in soul. It is to be a saint a most holy thing before God. It is to be warm, pure from every fault, carnality, to be modest, and clean. *Hagiazō* is to nurture with tender care.

From this, it is evident that *sanctification* is a separation process. It distinguishes something from the wicked, ordinary, or irreligious. What is amazing to realize is that God himself underwent and undergoes the process of sanctification.

"Thus will I magnify myself, and sanctify myself; and I will be known in the eyes of many nations, and they shall know that I am the LORD." Ezekiel 38:23

God informs Ezekiel that he will cause himself to be hallowed. He will be known as holy. People will learn how he is distinct from others. They will be able to recognize him, perceive and discriminate between his ways and other ways. They will be able to discern between the spiritual and the natural. Because God sanctified himself, nations would know that he is Jehovah.

Since Jesus saw Jehovah sanctify himself, he too had to sanctify himself (John 5:19). Christ sanctified himself as an obedient son but also for our sakes. Because he sanctified himself, it opened the way for us to be sanctified through him (truth).

"And for their sakes I sanctify myself, that they also might be sanctified through the truth." John 17:19

"Jesus saith unto him, I am the way, the truth, and the life: no man cometh unto the Father, but by me." John 14:6

Therefore, it is clear that if we refuse to be separate from the profane we are not true sons of God. Jehovah set the standard for holiness therefore it cannot change.

"Heaven and earth shall pass away, but my words shall not pass away." Matthew 24:35

"But the word of the Lord endureth for ever. And this is the word which by the

gospel is preached unto you." 1 Peter
1:25

"The grass withereth, the flower fadeth:
but the word of our God shall stand for
ever." Isaiah 40:8

Jehovah is wholly separate and
distinct from evil.

"To shew that the LORD is upright: he is
my rock, and there is no unrighteousness
in him." Psalm 92:15

All that he does is wholly good, absent
of wickedness, and void of corruption.
Therefore, his plans for his creation is
rooted, grounded, nurtured, and
implemented by the virtue of his
goodness.

"For I know the thoughts that I think
toward you, saith the LORD, thoughts of
peace, and not of evil, to give you an
expected end." Jeremiah 29:11

"And the very God of peace sanctify you
wholly; and I pray God your whole spirit
and soul and body be preserved

blameless unto the coming of our Lord Jesus Christ." 1 Thessalonians 5:23

The end that Jehovah has for all his sons is one that establishes hallowedness. One that makes it known that he is God and Jesus is Lord. Although sanctification is the plan of God, we must be willing to submit to the process. We are to present to God our living, breathing bodies as a victim in order to be kept safe from the danger of destruction. When we do this, we establish his holiness in our members. The presentation of our bodies to God is not a one-time event. It is a continual process in order to save us from perishing.

"I beseech you therefore, brethren, by the mercies of God, that ye present your bodies a living sacrifice, holy, acceptable unto God, which is your reasonable service." Romans 12:1

Sanctification opens the way for restoration and deliverance. It removes us from the snare of the enemy and places us in the safe hands of Jehovah *the God of peace.* Our separation from worldly living should be as clear as Sabbath worship was and is to a Jewish person. It is this mark or line of difference that will establish whose we are and what we truly believe.

"Moreover also I gave them my Sabbaths, to be a sign between me and them that they might know that I am the LORD that sanctify them." Ezekiel 20:12

DAY 17

GOD'S WORD IS LOVE

"He that loveth not knoweth not God; for God is love." 1 John 4:8

"And we have known and believed the love that God hath to us. God is love; and he that dwelleth in love dwelleth in God, and God in him." 1 John 4:16

The world that we live in is a twisted place. It labels what is wrong as right and what is right as wrong. Those who stand on the side of the Lord are considered fanatics, insensitive, or archaic. If you follow the commands of God, you are despised by the world and an offense to many.

"Woe unto them that call evil good, and good evil; that put darkness for light, and light for darkness; that put bitter for sweet, and sweet for bitter!" Isaiah 5:20

The opponents of the gospel or the enemies of God murmur with loud voices for they do not comprehend that every word that comes out of the mouth of God resonates with love. It was conceived in love, it was grown and birthed in love, and his words are love. Therefore, they reject it because they are unfamiliar with God's style of love.

The root of God's love is his friendliness toward us. All that he says and does is for the expressed purpose of wishing us well and doing well toward us. In every situation or circumstance, God intends it to work out for our good and spiritual benefit.

Why does God invest so much in us? He is fond of doing good and it pleases him to express his love! Jehovah is a God of signs and wonders. To that end, he continually displays signs of love toward us. God gave his words to men out of love. He sent Jesus to manifest that love in the flesh thus; he made it evident that his words are to befriend us in a relationship or covenantal love.

The word **agapaō** is the root word for **love** (**agapē**). *Agapaō* reveals God's fondness toward us. It discloses the truth that he loves us dearly. Therefore, he cannot act in a way that would betray his love toward us.

What is interesting is that God sanctioned his love toward us according to the word **phileō**, which is the root word for *agapaō*. To sanction is to give official authorization or agreement for an action. Therefore, God has consented to love us and he has agreed with himself to implement this love.

Each time we disobey God's Word we reject his love. God is love, his words are love therefore to accept his love we must obey his words.

"If ye love me, keep my commandments."
John 14:15

"Jesus answered and said unto him, If a man love me, he will keep my words: and my Father will love him, and we will come unto him, and make our abode with him." John 14:23

GOD'S WORD IS *SPIRITUAL* TRUTH

"Sanctify them through thy truth: thy word is truth." John 17:17

"For the word of the LORD is right; and all his works are done in truth." Psalm 33:4

Hear ye, hear ye people of God. Jehovah's Word is truth. It alone is true in any matter under deliberation! The Greek word **alētheia** is used in John 17:17 for the word **truth**. It means that by the standard of truth God's Word is true no matter what. Whether it pertains to the duties of men, morality, religion, or God the standard of truth is Jehovah's truth. Truth is the personal excellence of God. God's truth has honesty of mind that is free from pretense, falsehood, deceit, affection, or simulation. The truth of God is uncorrupted.

Alētheia gets its root meaning from the word **alēthēs** which reveals that God's Word is a loving the truth which is not hidden or concealed. The word **lanthanō** means to be hidden from one, to be unawares, or without knowing. As members of God's family, we are called to know him therefore; truth is not hidden from us.

The beginning of truth is God. Therefore, if we are to be rooted in truth we must believe that he is God.

"But without faith it is impossible to please him: for he that cometh to God must believe that he is, and that he is a rewarder of them that diligently seek him." Hebrews 11:6

"And this is life eternal, that they might know thee the only true God, and Jesus Christ, whom thou hast sent." John 17:3

Once we believe that he is God then the process of grounding us in truth can progress. Being filled with the knowledge of his will advances us in deeper truth for it opens the way for all wisdom and spiritual understanding. It will establish us in truth no matter what the discussion.

"For this cause we also, since the day we heard it, do not cease to pray for you, and to desire that ye might be filled with the knowledge of his will in all wisdom and spiritual understanding;" Colossians 1:9

"That the God of our Lord Jesus Christ, the Father of glory, may give unto you the spirit of wisdom and revelation in the knowledge of him:" Ephesians 1:17

When we abide in truth, we have to love for God's truth is loving always.

"He that loveth not knoweth not God; for God is love." 1 John 4:8

"In this the children of God are manifest, and the children of the devil: whosoever doeth not righteousness is not of God,

neither he that loveth not his brother." 1 John 3:10

Truth demands love for they are woven together. One cannot exist without the other. The Word of God is *spiritual* truth for God is a spirit and his Word possesses the nature of God.

"God is a Spirit: and they that worship him must worship him in spirit and in truth." John 4:24

As his offspring, we are called to live in and by the spiritual breath of God. Holy Spirit the Spirit of Truth is to be our inhalation and exhalation. He reveals the true Word of God to us. If we listen to him, we will remain grounded in truth. If we allow him to show us, what is to come we will be prepared and ready in all situations.

"Howbeit when he, the Spirit of truth, is come, he will guide you into all truth: for he shall not speak of himself; but whatsoever he shall hear, that shall he speak: and he will shew you things to come." John 16:13

"He shall glorify me: for he shall receive of mine, and shall shew it unto you."
John 16:14

DAY 19

GOD'S WORD TEACHES

"For everything that was written in the past was written for our instruction, so that through endurance and the encouragement of the Scriptures, we might have hope." Romans 15:4

Jehovah's words are meant to explain, teach, or expound on a matter. When we read his words, they instruct us. The word **instruction** in Romans 15:4 reveal to us the God's purpose for writing his words down. **Didaskalia** is the Greek word for instruction it means doctrine, teaching, precepts, or something taught.

Didaskalia gets its root meaning from the word **didaskalos**, which means a teacher. *Didaskalos* gets its meaning from the word **didaskō**, which means to instill doctrine, to operate as a teacher, or to impart instruction. Therefore, woven into the meaning of *instruction* is the function and responsibility of a teacher, which is to instill doctrine.

The Word of God imparts, drills, implants, and introduces precepts. It also helps us know the doctrines of God. The subtle implication is that in order for God's Word to teach us we must be willing to be his student. We must understand that our lives are a classroom. Our lessons occur continually day and night. The school of God is **never** out of session. *There are no breaks* therefore; we need to be willing to learn at all times, in or out of season.

The remarkable thing about God's Word is that it teaches truth. As disciples of Christ we are not above him. We will be exposed to the same things that he went through. Men will mock and ridicule us. They will say all manner of evil against us (Matthew 5:11-12). They called Christ the lord of flies, Beelzebub. Therefore, what will they say about us?

"It is enough for the disciple that he be as his master, and the servant as his lord. If they have called the master of the house Beelzebub, how much more shall they call them of his household?" Matthew 10:25

"The disciple is not above his master: but every one that is perfect shall be as his master." Luke 6:40

God teaches us the truth about the challenges we will face as we walk with Christ. He has hidden nothing. We are to weigh the cost for ourselves and choose wisely (Luke 14:25-34). Unlike worldly teachers, God provides the benefits of living by his Word as well as those things that are disquieting about following him completely.

"All scripture is given by inspiration of God, and is profitable for doctrine, for reproof, for correction, for instruction in righteousness:" 2 Timothy 3:16

There is a cost to righteousness. Christ paid the ultimate cost. However, there is also a multitude of blessings to being instructed in right living. We must choose which one is most important to us. Saving our natural lives at the cost of our eternal life or laying down our soulish nature in order to gain a spiritual one.

"For whosoever will save his life shall lose it: and whosoever will lose his life for my sake shall find it." Matthew 16:25

DAY 20

GOD'S WORD EQUIPS FOR GOOD WORKS

"All scripture is given by inspiration of God, and is profitable for doctrine, for reproof, for correction, for instruction in righteousness: That the man of God may be perfect, thoroughly furnished unto all good works." 2 Timothy 3:16-17

God's Word is all powerful. It is a mighty weapon, a teacher; it is a legal document, purifier, discerner, and a lamp. An instrument that fashions us unto good works. What does God consider good works? Does he evaluate good works as we do?

Agathos is the word for ***good***. It means useful, agreeable, excellent, honorable, distinguished, pleasant, and of good constitution or nature. To do *good* is to distinguish oneself, to outshine in any respect, and to bear the fruits of goodness. Uprightness is the ability to fulfill a responsibility or a service. The Word of God enables us to have a relationship with a "positive standard," with "moral goodness," and with righteousness. When we honor and conform to the standard of God then the works we do will be labeled as *good.* In all, that we do the assessment of men is irrelevant. When it comes to goodness there is only one judge and he will not ask others to cast their vote on our behalf.

Ergon is the word for works. It means employment, enterprise, undertaking, or business. *Ergon* is anything done, any act, or deed with which we are occupied. What this indicates is that our lives are to be the fertile soil from which good works spring. Good works are not limited to church activities. Or family obligations. It is not just about serving at the food pantry or donating to the poor. Opportunities for good works lay all around us. Being polite while riding on the train. Saying good morning to a stranger. Blessing

someone who cut you off on the road.
Speaking correction to a wayward
child in love.

Without God's Word it is impossible to
achieve good works. God's Word must
furnish us. *Exartizō* is the word for
furnish. It means to finish us
completely, to perfect us. It is to
complete us with "special aptitude for
given uses" according to the root
meaning *artios*. This is accomplished
when we allow God's Word to lift us
up, to elevate us, or to draw us up as
fish (*airō*). The Word of God is always
ready to accomplish its mission. It is
ready at this moment, at this time,
even right now. It is versatile for it can
confirm to any situation converting it
into something good.

*"And we know that all things work
together for good to them that love God,
to them who are the called according to
his purpose." Romans 8:28*

When we trust, believe, and rely on
God's Word then we **know** that all
things will work together for good. We

have an assurance that when we stand on the word of God truth is established, that we love the Lord, and that we are called according to his purpose.

"Now the God of peace, that brought again from the dead our Lord Jesus, that great shepherd of the sheep, through the blood of the everlasting covenant, Make you perfect in every good work to do his will, working in you that which is wellpleasing in his sight, through Jesus Christ; to whom be glory for ever and ever. Amen." Hebrews 13:20-21

May the Lord establish us in every good work by the power of his Word. May it be active and demonstrative in our lives, in the name of Jesus.

DAY 21

GOD'S WORD A WEAPON OF DIVISION

"For the word of God [is] quick, and powerful, and sharper than any twoedged sword, piercing even to the dividing asunder of soul and spirit, and of the joints and marrow, and [is] a discerner of the thoughts and intents of the heart." Hebrews 4:12

God has equipped believers with a mighty weapon, his Word. Jehovah's Word is able to bring about *division* between the soul and spirit and the joint and marrow. What does it mean to divide asunder? **Merismos** is the word used for the phrase **dividing asunder**. It means to separate, part, to cut in pieces or to split into fractions. As we investigate its root meaning, we find it means to section off in allotments or to assign to one.

Therefore, when we speak the Word of God we are equipped with the ability to cut in pieces and section off things for God.

It is curious that Paul mentioned specifically the soul and spirit and joints and marrow. What is the significance of these parts of our being? The soul is the part of us, which wanes in its love towards God. While the spirit is hot for the God of spirits (Romans 8:14, John 4:24). Therefore, God's Word will trim away anything that will cause us not to be on fire for him. It will help us to be in good health for it helps our souls to prosper in righteousness (Revelations 1:11, Revelations 2-3).

"Beloved, I wish above all things that thou mayest prosper and be in health, even as thy soul prospereth." 3 John 1:2

As our souls prosper in the ways of God, it opens the way for our bodies to exist in good health. The truth is our former lives were committed to sin (1Corinthians 618). Our souls enjoyed it and because of that many of the things that our bodies suffer is because of the deprivation of our souls. This is why God sent his word to separate us from our former soulish ways (thoughts, emotions, motives, and actions).

From the words in 3 John 1:2 we see that there is a connection between the flourishing of our physical bodies and the thriving of our souls. When our souls prosper, it will establish health for us. Likewise, when our souls decline in righteousness and truth it will affect the health of our bodies.

The Word of God divides the joint from marrow. This means it is able to sever anything that has joined itself to us or what we have joined ourselves to. Iniquity and sin adjoined themselves to us from the time of conception. They have created a joint and it is this joining that God's Word divides.

"Behold, I was shapen in iniquity; and in sin did my mother conceive me." Psalm 51:5

Harma is the root word for *harmos* (*joint*) it means chariot or armed war chariots. *Harma* gets its meaning from the word *airō* that means to rise up, lift up, or to elevate. Therefore, the intent of iniquity and sin is to elevate itself to a position of prominence above God. Their goal is to rob God of what is rightfully his. The objective of *airō* is to cause us to cease. While God's intent for us is eternal life or eternal existence.

Myelos is the Greek word for *marrow*. It means enclosed according to the Thayer's Greek Lexicon. It represents that which is shut up, closed, or within. God's Word is able to separate us even from those things that are not evident to others. Those things that are shut up within us, hidden things, things that can defile us.

"And he said, That which cometh out of the man, that defileth the man. For from within, out of the heart of men, proceed evil thoughts, adulteries, fornications, murders, Thefts, covetousness, wickedness, deceit, lasciviousness, an

evil eye, blasphemy, pride, foolishness:
All these evil things come from within,
and defile the man." Mark 7:20-23

His Word is able to penetrate the core of our being. The secret places where sin and iniquity have made their habitation. It is able to establish a line that divides them from us and us from them. It is able to break them in pieces and expose them as mere parlor tricks before a powerful God.

DAY 22

GOD'S WORD IS A DISCERNER OF THOUGHTS

"For the word of God [is] quick, and powerful, and sharper than any twoedged sword, piercing even to the dividing asunder of soul and spirit, and of the joints and marrow, and [is] a discerner of the thoughts and intents of the heart." Hebrews 4:12

Jehovah's Word is a discerner of thoughts. What does it mean to be a discerner? *Kritikos* is the Greek word used for discerner. It means to be skilled in judging. God's Word is fit to judge. It is able to be an arbiter. He takes for himself judgement.

"There is one lawgiver, who is able to save and to destroy: who art thou that judgest another?" James 4:12

"But God is the judge: he putteth down one, and setteth up another." Psalm 75:7

God's Word separates, picks out, approves, determines, decrees, and resolves. His Word is fit to rule and govern. It settles disputes, and contends with opposers in a forensic sense. All that the word of God does as it discerns is summed up in the Greek word **krinō**.

When we live according to the Bible, we are able to judge matters as God would. It strips away our biases and prejudices. The only thing that is relevant is God's view of the matter. His Word purifies our motives, it focuses our attention on the will of God, and it allows us to rightly judge matters.

Paul lived according to the Word of the Lord. He agreed with God and consented to the ways of God. He allowed the mind of Christ to be established in him. Therefore when a delicate matter arose in the Corinthian church he did not hesitate to judge based on his knowledge and agreement with the standard of God.

"I wrote unto you in an epistle not to company with fornicators: Yet not altogether with the fornicators of this world, or with the covetous, or extortioners, or with idolaters; for then must ye needs go out of the world. But now I have written unto you not to keep company, if any man that is called a brother be a fornicator, or covetous, or an idolater, or a railer, or a drunkard, or an extortioner; with such an one no not to eat. For what have I to do to judge them also that are without? do not ye judge them that are within? But them that are without God judgeth. Therefore put away from among yourselves that wicked person." 1 Corinthians 5:9-13

As children of God, we are called to uphold his standard. We are to judge as God has judged. If a brother is struggling, we are to encourage and support him. But if our brother is reveling in sin and refuses to repent we are to cut him off for his sin will be like cancer to the children of God.

A man aspiring for righteousness will call his sin a sin. On the other hand, one who is on a downward decent will rationalize and excuse his sin. He will say, "None of us are perfect. I'm only human. Everyone else is doing it or worse." This individual does not rightly discern the standard or expectation of God for his children. **Holiness is not optional for a son of God**—*it is required*.

"Because it is written, Be ye holy; for I am holy." 1 Peter 1:16

There is to be a mark of distinction between us and the world. Between their nature and ours. If that mark is not there then we are not walking according to the standard of God. The ability to uphold the ways of God comes by applying his Word to our lives and establishing his judgments in all matters as our own including our thoughts.

Enthymēsis is the Greek word for **thoughts**. It means thinking or considering. It involves anything that is brought to mind, things that we deliberate upon, or ponder about. It is any issue, which we are trying to resolve in our mind. It includes things that cause us to become angry, passionate, or heated.

No matter what we are, struggling with the Word is fit to help us make the right decision each and every time. For it cuts past the irrelevant arguments and highlights the core issues as God sees it.

The Word of God is Jesus. The source of wisdom is Jesus. Who do we need to help us discern correctly in every matter?

"If any of you lack wisdom, let him ask of God, that giveth to all men liberally, and upbraideth not; and it shall be given him." James 1:5

"But of him are ye in Christ Jesus, who of God is made unto us wisdom, and righteousness, and sanctification, and redemption:" 1 Corinthians 1:30

Jesus!

DAY 23

GOD'S WORD DISCERNS INTENTS OF THE HEART

"For the word of God [is] quick, and powerful, and sharper than any twoedged sword, piercing even to the dividing asunder of soul and spirit, and of the joints and marrow, and [is] a discerner of the thoughts and intents of the heart." Hebrews 4:12

Intent according to the Merriam-Webster Dictionary Online is "the state of mind with which an act is done." It is a clearly formulated plan of intent. The Greek word **ennoia** reveals that intent means the act of thinking, meditation, or considering. It is a notion or conception. It involves a manner of feeling. Developing intentions utilizes our intellect it requires understanding, and perception. It is to reason in a *narrower* sense. To operate in spiritual truth in higher realms of understanding and power.

In order to ascend to higher levels in our formulation of intents we need the Word of God otherwise our goals are of substandard caliber. God desires that our hearts are full of sober judgments. Judgments that is calm and impartial in nature. God is fashioning us to be like him.

"For there is no respect of persons with God." Romans 2:11

"Then Peter opened his mouth, and said, Of a truth I perceive that God is no respecter of persons:" Acts 10:34

"For the LORD your God is God of gods, and Lord of lords, a great God, a mighty, and a terrible, which regardeth not persons, nor taketh reward:" Deuteronomy 10:17

"How much less to him that accepteth not the persons of princes, nor regardeth

*the rich more than the poor? for they all
are the work of his hands." Job 34:19*

The Word of God Jesus will help to
establish the right desires within our
hearts.

*"Delight thyself also in the LORD; and he
shall give thee the desires of thine heart."
Psalm 37:4*

Naturally, our hearts are wicked
therefore, without the help of God our
desires are corrupt (Jeremiah 17:9). In
order to have pure desires God has to
give us a heart transplant (Ezekiel
36:26, Ezekiel 11:19). The new heart of
God is undivided and it is full of the
spirit of Jehovah. Therefore, it will
long to do what pleases him. It will
crave after what he craves after. It will
long for his will and purposes to be
fulfilled in every situation. It will by
default want to please him. Only the
heart fashioned by God will be
pleasant unto Jehovah.

God's Word not only establishes the
right desires within us it also exposed

those things that are in opposition to the will of God. It exposes unforgiveness, hatred, lust, pride, and every other thing that defiles (1 Timothy 1:8-15). Hi Word washes us, removes immorality, falsehood, idolatry, and multitude of other sins (Revelation 22:14-17).

What does God desire? He wants us to be without spot, blemish, or wrinkle (Ephesians 5:27). He desires truth to be established in our inward parts.

"Behold, thou desirest truth in the inward parts: and in the hidden part thou shalt make me to know wisdom."
Psalm 51:6

Truth can only be established by the source of truth, which is Jesus. He is the only way for truth to be officially fixed within us. Furthermore, it is the only way for us to receive life rooted in truth.

If we allow the Word to examine our hearts, he will establish truth within us. He will give life unto us and he will set up his throne within us. From our heart, he will govern our appetites, passions, affections, emotions, endeavors, desires, and purposes. He will be seated at the center of our physical and spiritual lives establishing good in all that concerns us.

DAY 24

GOD'S WORD IS QUICK

"For the word of God [is] quick, and powerful, and sharper than any twoedged sword, piercing even to the dividing asunder of soul and spirit, and of the joints and marrow, and [is] a discerner of the thoughts and intents of the heart." Hebrews 4:12

The things that God's Word can do is simply amazing. It possesses no deficiencies. It is capable of addressing all needs, wants, concerns, and situations. It is also able to do so immediately with an element of speed. Why?

God's word is **quick**. His word is **zaō**. *Zaō* means to be alive, to live, to be among the living as opposed to the lifeless or the dead. It is to be worthy of the name and to possess *true* life for it is to breathe. Hidden in *zaō* is power, activity, and vital power within itself.

Zaō exposes to our understanding his Word is alive. It is worthy of the name life or living. It is strong and powerful. It is fresh and efficient. If we allow God's Word to be active in our lives, it will cause us to breathe spiritual air. It will usher in spiritual life. It will use its power on our behalf. It will enable us to enjoy **real life**.

What is *real life*? The life that God intended for us from the beginning. Lives that are rooted and ground in him. Lives that please and delight him. Lives that crown him with glory. Lives that are devoid of darkness.

God's Word was dispatched from heaven to divide the inhabitants into the quick and the dead. Jesus (the Word of God) will ultimately judge us for how we respond to the invitation of God and how we complete the process of God.

"And he commanded us to preach unto the people, and to testify that it is he which was ordained of God to be the Judge of quick and dead." Acts 10:42

"I charge thee therefore before God, and the Lord Jesus Christ, who shall judge the quick and the dead at his appearing and his kingdom;" 2 Timothy 4:1

"Who shall give account to him that is ready to judge the quick and the dead." 1 Peter 4:5

The Word of God is able to accomplish its mission, which is to produce replicas of Jesus throughout the earth. We are to be *quick* possessing the breath of God within us. We are to be mighty men and women for the most high. We are to be strong and able to enjoy *real life* as God has defined it. We are to be blessed, active, and continuous for the kingdom of God. Meaning that whatever we sow is to outlive our natural lives and continue to produce a harvest into eternity (Jeremiah 35:1-19).

His Word has come to separate us from among the dead. We have been called to dwell with life and among the living. What business do we have among the dead except to call them into life? May we learn to be *quick* as the Word of God!

DAY 25

GOD'S WORD PURIFIES

"Is not my word like as a fire? saith the LORD; and like a hammer that breaketh the rock in pieces?" Jeremiah 23:29

What is the purpose of fire? What is its significance? In the natural realm, fire is a catalyst for necessary change. Often fires remove foreign plants that compete with native species for space and nutrients. It removes undergrowth that opens the way for sunlight to reach the woodland surface. Fires help to encourage new growth in forests. Fires are often considered bad, but they play a pivotal role in renewing the forest.

"'Wherefore thus saith the LORD God of hosts, Because ye speak this word, behold, I will make my words in thy

mouth fire, and this people wood, and it shall devour them." Jeremiah 5:14

God's Word is like a fire for the forest of our lives. Foreign species have invaded the territory and they need to be ruthlessly removed. In order for us to thrive in the kingdom of Jehovah, his light must be able to reach the core of our being.

If we allow it, his Word will renew us. It will cause the native species of Christ's character to spring forth within us thus achieving its purpose to the glory of God.

There are things; however, that fire is unable to destroy. It may singe, disfigure, or melt it, but it does not utterly destroy it. Some of these things can be repurposed in the hands of God. Their value does not lie in their current state, but in what they can become in the hands of the Master Craftsman.

Likewise, in our lives there are somethings that may be so hardened that it requires something other than fire. This is why God's word is like a hammer. It is able to pound or continually assault until it changes the nature, shape, and purpose of a thing.

God desires to use us as he did the prophets of old. He is fashioning us after his likeness. In order for us to be effective, we have to go through the process.

"Therefore have I hewed them by the prophets; I have slain them by the words of my mouth: and thy judgments are as the light that goeth forth." Hosea 6:5

As fire, the Word of God has a multitude of purposes. God uses it to put fire in the mouth and bones of his people (Jeremiah 1:9, Jeremiah 20:9). It is a source of heat for us. It keeps us passionate and zealous for the Lord. It prevents us from growing cold (Revelation 3:15-17). If we find ourselves growing cold to the things of God, it is a good indication that we are not allowing him to fill us with the fire of his Word.

God purifies where he desires to build. He removes the evidence of the enemy. He demolishes old structures and strongholds (Proverbs 9:1). He salvages material that he deems useful. What we may consider beneficial to him may not be profitable to God at all. He methodically lays the foundation in light. He builds upon it brick by brick. Some bricks may need to be chiseled or smoothened. While other may need to be reduced in size or specially cut to fit the location God has designated.

"Ye also, as lively stones, are built up a spiritual house, an holy priesthood, to offer up spiritual sacrifices, acceptable to God by Jesus Christ." 1 Peter 2:5

When stones are exposed to light, they get hot. The heat they capture lasts for hours. Likewise as stones of God, we are to exist in the heat of his presence. We are to acknowledge that abiding in *fire* is a requirement to walking with our God.

"This then is the message which we have heard of him, and declare unto you, that God is light, and in him is no darkness at all." 1 John 1:5

"For our God is a consuming fire." Hebrews 12:29

DAY 26

THE WORD OF GOD IS A JUDGE

"He that rejecteth me, and receiveth not my words, hath one that judgeth him: the word that I have spoken, the same shall judge him in the last day." John 12:48

God's Word is *fit* for the work assigned to it. It is able to meet every need, tear down strongholds, separate us from the enemy and the enemy from us. It is also able to train us in righteous judgement.

Jehovah's words enable is to better judge our lives and the situations we face in this life. It prepares us for our future role as judges of angels.

"Know ye not that we shall judge angels? how much more things that pertain to this life?" 1 Corinthians 6:3

However, before we can judge angels the Word of God will judge us. Every word that the Father has spoken. Each word that the Son has shared. Every word that Holy Spirit has made known unto us will judge us. What does the judgment process entail?

The word **krinō** is used for judgeth. It is to separate, select, pluck out, or to choose. It is to prefer one to another or to deem one fit and another not. The Word of God will sift us like cattle before his throne. It will decide which of us are worthy to enter into the rest of the Lord and which ones are not.

When we stand before God, his Word will preside over us and it will examine us. Forensically speaking his Word will possess all the evidence either to vindicate us or to pronounce us guilty. God's Words are not just mere words on a page or grand speeches spoken from a pulpit. Jesus is the Word of God and he is our advocate. He is the one who petitions God on our behalf. He is the one who resides within us.

"My little children, these things write I unto you, that ye sin not. And if any man sin, we have an advocate with the Father, Jesus Christ the righteous:" 1 *John 2:1*

"Jesus answered and said unto him, If a man love me, he will keep my words: and my Father will love him, and we will come unto him, and make our abode with him." John 14:23

As our *advocate*, he publically supports us and presents our cause to the Father by recommending intervention because of the stripes he took and the blood he shed. As our *supporter*, he is intimately acquainted with us. He knows what we know, what we do not know, and what we could or should have known. Since he is infallible and incorruptible his testimony for or against us will be beyond reproach. Therefore, when he speaks no one can dispute the soundness of his judgment.

The Greek word for advocate is *paraklētos* it means one who is called to a person's aid. One who is an intercessor, a helper, or an assistant. An advocate is a pleader, a legal assistant, or counsel for the defense. Jesus is all of these for us. In this season, he is advocating for us to be free from the traps of the enemy, to be reconciled to God, for every mark and blemish of the enemy to be removed, and for God to pour out his grace to meet our needs. However, the time is coming when Christ will be an advocate to enforce the standard of God throughout heaven and earth. If we are willing, he will get us ready by the soundness of God's Word.

DAY 27

GOD'S WORD BREATHES

"It is the spirit that quickeneth; the flesh profiteth nothing: the words that I speak unto you, they are spirit, and they are life." John 6:63

The spirit of Christ is the source of *real life* (Romans 8:9). It quickens *all* who receive it. To **quicken** is to produce alive in the sense of giving birth to live offspring. It is to bear living young. The Word of God is also able to restore life as in giving the dying or unconscious CPR (cardiopulmonary resuscitation). It can also raise the dead causing them to *spring* to life.

Human beings need to take in and breathe out air in order to live. Likewise, our spirit man requires the spiritual air of God in order to remain alive. *Spiritual* breath is needed in order for us to thrive and prosper in *life* as God ordained it.

Once equipped with the spirit of Christ our souls begin to undergo a process of becoming prosperous.

"Beloved, I wish above all things that thou mayest prosper and be in health, even as thy soul prospereth." 3 John 1:2

Our ability to prosper in life and to be in good health is intrinsically linked to the prosperity of our souls.

The Greek word soul is **psyche** it means breath of life. *Psyche* gets its core meaning from the word **psychō**, which means to blow, to grow cold or waning love. This indicates that the natural condition or state of our soul is to be cold or to possess diminished love toward man and certainly toward God.

Therefore, when John shared his wish for the brethren to prosper in all things as their soul prospered he revealed the heart and intent of God. The origin of his words was love and its foundation was truth (3 John 1:1).

Without the Word of God (spirit of Christ), our souls will not prosper. Only God's Word is able to quicken the soul of men. For *only* his breath is able to produce live offspring. His breath *alone* is able to resurrect the dead.

We were once dead and because of his Word, because of his spirit our souls have been quickened.

DAY 28

GOD'S WORD IS CLEANSING

"That he might sanctify and cleanse it with the washing of water by the word,"
Ephesians 5:26

To cleanse is to make something completely clean. To remove defiling properties, to eliminate unpleasant traits, to remove unwanted entities. It is to free someone from guilt or sin.

The process of cleansing according to the word **katharos** is to make pure by fire or pruning. It is to be unstained by guilt, to be free of corrupt desires, and to be completely clean. It is to be blameless.

God's Word has the power to accomplish this in the lives of his children. In fact, God has declared that he is preparing a company of people (the Church) who will possess this very nature.

His Word enables us to do what we cannot do on our own. Our submission to his Word will transform us into pure and blameless children of God.

"That you may be blameless and harmless, the sons of God, without rebuke, in the midst of a crooked and perverse nation, among whom you shine as lights in the world; Holding forth the word of life; that I may rejoice in the day of Christ, that I have not run in vain, neither laboured in vain." Philippians 2:15-16

Let us not deceive ourselves God is not looking for our goodness to be established he requires that his goodness be established within us. He does not want us to clean ourselves because we cannot! He has assigned that task to his Word. He has given that task to the spirit of Christ.

DAY 29

GOD'S WORD IS A SEED

"Now the parable is this: The seed is the word of God." Luke 8:11

In Luke 8, Christ shares a parable of a sower who went out to sow seeds. Some of his seeds fell by the wayside. Some were eaten by fowls or trodden under foot. Other seed fell on a rock and withered because they did not get the moisture needed to survive. Some fell among thorns, which choked the life out of them. However, others fell on good ground, sprang up, and bore abundant fruit.

The disciples did not understand the significance of the seeds until Jesus shared with them the nature and purpose of God's Word. Many will hear the Word of God, but it will only bear fruit in the lives of a few. Some from the beginning will hear the God's Word and discard it. Treating it carelessly with neglect and insult as if trampling it under their feet. Daily they will go through life not giving the Word of God any thought or consideration as they routinely do as they have always done.

For the ones who do not cast the Word aside the enemy will dispatch workers (fowls) who will swoop in to devour the seed. These creatures will use the cares of life to rob the hearer of the precious Word of God. They will inflict injuries, overwhelm them with strong emotions, and they will sap them of bodily strength. Their objective is to suck life out of them, to deplete their substance before they are able to understand or believe the Word of God.

Others will hear the Word and it will begin to bud. These individuals will not seek moisture therefore what started to grow will dry up and die. Leaving their hearts (souls), hardened depriving them of the new life offered by God.

The other group will fall among plants, which are prickly. Plants which are growing in the same area, but are fighting against their survival. This indicates that it will be a violent relationship for each is fighting for space, desiring to survive, and competing for an opportunity to establish itself. Jesus let his disciples know that those who are found among the thorns will perish for life will be choked out of them.

The story will be different for those whose seed falls on good ground. Those who refuse to insult God by casting away his Word are cultivating good ground. Those who refuse to allow their souls to continue in an unrejuvenated state are plowing the ground of their hearts.

Anyone who sets a watch over the Word of God that they have received will prevent satanic fowls from devouring the precious word they have received. Awareness of the worth of the God's Word helps to prepare the ground of our lives for proper spiritual growth.

Those who find themselves among thorns and seeks God will be delivered (Luke 22:44, 1 Corinthians 10:13). However, those who choose to weather it alone without the help of God will succumb to the highest pressure that the enemy will inflict.

Jehovah's Word is not only a seed but it also is a warning to those who hear it. It reveals what is to come if we are not mindful or careful. The parable of the sower exposes all the hidden dangers that are lurking to make God's Word unprofitable in our lives. In order to prosper in life we need to his Word. In order for God's Word to do its work we must be willing to utilize it to plow the fields of our hearts, influence the course of our souls, and alter the state of our minds. It will teach us how to rely on God and grow in him through obedience.

"Though he were a Son, yet learned he obedience by the things which he suffered; And being made perfect, he became the author of eternal salvation unto all them that obey him;" Hebrews 5:8-9

DAY 30

GOD'S WORD IS A POWERFUL FORCE

"So shall my word be that goeth forth out of my mouth: it shall not return unto me void, but it shall accomplish that which I please, and it shall prosper in the thing whereto I sent it." Isaiah 55:11

When rain or snow falls to the earth they bring forth growth and increase in the land. They fall in order to bless those who sow and those who eat. Likewise, the Word of God is dispatched with purpose. It is formulated for growth and nourishment. As snow and rain do not return to the heavens without accomplishing their tasks neither does the Word of God. Neither rain nor snow can defy the natural order of things nor can the Word of the Lord. It must accomplish what it is sent to do!

In Genesis, we are told of the flood, which was started by rain.

"For yet seven days, and I will cause it to rain upon the earth forty days and forty nights; and every living substance that I have made will I destroy from off the face of the earth." Genesis 7:4

The rain was so powerful that it destroyed the earth.

"And God said unto Noah, The end of all flesh is come before me; for the earth is filled with violence through them; and, behold, I will destroy them with the earth." Genesis 6:13

Rain can be a destructive force when it is unleashed without measure by God.

"And I will establish my covenant with you; neither shall all flesh be cut off any more by the waters of a flood; neither shall there any more be a flood to destroy the earth." Genesis 9:11

In the same vain, it accomplishes its task when it is sent to water crops, to correct the wayward, or to destroy the guilty according to the purpose of God (Ezekiel 13:13).

God keeps the storehouses of snow and of hail. They are at his disposal and they fulfill his purposes in the earth.

"Hast thou entered into the treasures of the snow? or hast thou seen the treasures of the hail, Which I have reserved against the time of trouble, against the day of battle and war?" Job 38:22-23

God uses the elements of his creation not only to bless but for battle. He uses them in order to win wars.

"The LORD is a man of war: the LORD is his name." Exodus 15:3

The Lord is a warrior. He goes forth with might and strength (Ezekiel 25:17).

"The LORD shall go forth as a mighty man, he shall stir up jealousy like a man of war: he shall cry, yea, roar; he shall prevail against his enemies." Isaiah 42:13

God is training us after his likeness (Ephesians 6:11-13, 3:8). He wants us fit for battle. It is for this reason that he sent us his word in three ways: the written word, the manifested word (Jesus) and the word through the spirit of Christ (Holy Spirit). God has thought of every possible scenarios which could derail our progress and he has sent forth provision.

God's Word will `*asah* (*accomplish*) his will. It will fashion, produce, will do the work necessary, and it will deal with anything that interferes with the process. His word will put all in order; it will bring about all that he has ordained. God's Word will observe the will of God and celebrate him.

"Faithful is he that calleth you, who also will do it." 1 Thessalonians 5:24

*"If we believe not, yet he abideth
faithful: he cannot deny himself." 2
Timothy 2:13*

God's Word must perform what it is
sent to do because it cannot deny the
One who sent it.

God's Word is not lazy. It cannot just
do the task. It must establish God's
superiority in the matter. It must
exhibit his nature and his character.
God does nothing with an element of
lack or insufficiency. Therefore, his
Word must demonstrate its power to
be profitable, to succeed, to progress
no matter what.

God's Word will **tsalach (prosper)** by
passing through or crossing over.
Tsalach is to attach or to fall upon.
God's Word has the ability to penetrate
anything that stands in its way until it
pierces through to the other side.

Christ was pierced for our rebellion. He
was crushed because of our sins. This
is why the Word of God is able to pass
through any barrier or obstruction the

enemy puts up whether naturally or physically.

"But he was wounded for our transgressions, he was bruised for our iniquities: the chastisement of our peace was upon him; and with his stripes we are healed." Isaiah 53:5

The Word of the Lord is able to pierce through to bring healing and restoration to us if we believe and utilize his Word by faith (Hebrews 11:6).

The objective of God's Word is to cause us to finish well.

"Wherefore seeing we also are compassed about with so great a cloud of witnesses, let us lay aside every weight, and the sin which doth so easily beset us, and let us run with patience the race that is set before us, Looking unto Jesus the author and finisher of our faith; who for the joy that was set before him endured the cross, despising the shame, and is set down at the right hand of the throne of God." Hebrews 12:1-2

Jehovah desires that each of us will be able to declare that we have finished the race and kept the faith. However, that is only accomplished by the power of God's Word (Jesus) in our lives.

"I have fought a good fight, I have finished my course, I have kept the faith:" 2 Timothy 4:7

The Word of God has exited the mouth of God. It was released to into the earth in order to lead us out and to deliver us from slavery. God's Word will set us on a course of advancement in the kingdom of God. It will cause us to go forward and never backward. It is infused with purpose and is guaranteed to yield a result.

What we choose to do with God's Word is up to us. God's Word lacks nothing! If we fall short, it is not because of a deficiency in the Word but rather a lack of practical and faithful application of the Word.

God has sent the force of his Word to be with us. Will we allow it to help us finish the course set before us?

CONCLUSION

Father, we thank you that you have sent your Word to be an aid to us. We bless you for opening our eyes to the power and might of your Word.

It is fit, able, and competent to do all that you desire to do in our lives. Help us to trust you. Help us to rely on your Word. Help us to rest patiently in you, in the name of Jesus.

Help us to understand every aspect of your word. Its nature, its character and its purpose on a new level. Open our eyes that we will see what we could not see before.

Lord, as you took the Children of Israel across the Jordan please cross us over from where we are to where we should be in the name of Jesus.

Father, we bless your name, amen.

Additional copies of this and other
books are available online at the
Createspace Store
http://createspace.com
under
M. J. Welcome
Michelle J. Dyett-Welcome

www.ingramcontent.com/pod-product-compliance
Lightning Source LLC
Chambersburg PA
CBHW031957040426
42448CB00006B/400